It's just different now

This book is about a boy named Henry.
His mum and dad have separated.

SPECTRUM PUBLICATIONS

First published in Australia in 1999
1st reprint 2003
2nd reprint 2009 with updated images
by Spectrum Publications Pty Ltd
PO Box 75, Richmond, Vic, 3121
Telephone: +61(3) 9415 9750
Facsimile: + 61(3) 9419 0783
spectrum@specrumpublications.com.au
www.spectrumpublications.com.au

Cover art: Gabrielle Greig

Cover design: Terry Callahan, Spectrum
Typesetting by Spectrum Publications

ISBN(10-dig) 0 86786 277 7
ISBN(13-dig) 978 0 86786 277 5

Author's Note to Adult Readers

It's Just Different Now is suitable for children between the ages of 3 and 7 years.

Grief is often only associated with experiences of death. It is important for us to recognise and acknowledge that grief is a process which is also experienced after many other situations that result in loss and change, such as family break-up.

Talking to children about parental separation and divorce is often difficult for adults and is sometimes overlooked or avoided. Often children struggle to understand and make sense of their feelings and reactions after family break-up. This book aims to facilitate careful listening, discussion and sharing between a trusted adult and a child.

It is important for children to hear and understand words like 'grief' and 'grieving', 'loss' and 'death'. During discussions with children, and in answering their questions, adults need to provide open and honest responses appropriate to the child's age and level of understanding.

It's Just Different Now will provide children with an opportunity to reflect on and talk about some of their thoughts, feelings and responses which are commonly associated with grief.

Grieving is unique for each individual. Like adults, children vary in the intensity and duration of their grief experience. Consequently, children will relate to the words and illustrations within this book differently, each in their own way.

Reading the story at a leisurely pace, discussing the illustrations and child's responses will assist adult readers in their understanding and support of the child's unique experience.

The illustrations in this book have been carefully developed using symbolic representation, enabling children to form their own images, summoning their unique story from within.

In addition to reading this book, adults may encourage children to use creative mediums such as painting, drawing and writing to further express their experience. These may or may not be shared with others, dependent on the child's wishes.

—Linda Espie

By the same author:
A to Z Reflections on Loss and Grief
Words (with Russell Deal)
Symbols (with Russell Deal)
Let the Children be our Teachers: A Guide for Japanese Professionals

Dedicated to all children who are grieving.

Henry's tummy felt funny.

Like it was full of butterflies.

His head felt wizzy.

Like it was busy with ants.

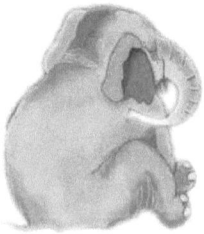

And every time he thought about his mum and dad

not living together anymore,

he felt something heavy on his heart.

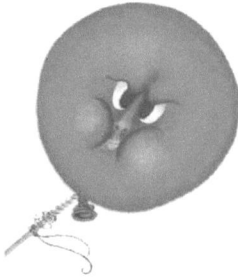

Sometimes Henry would get so angry

he'd feel like he was going to burst.

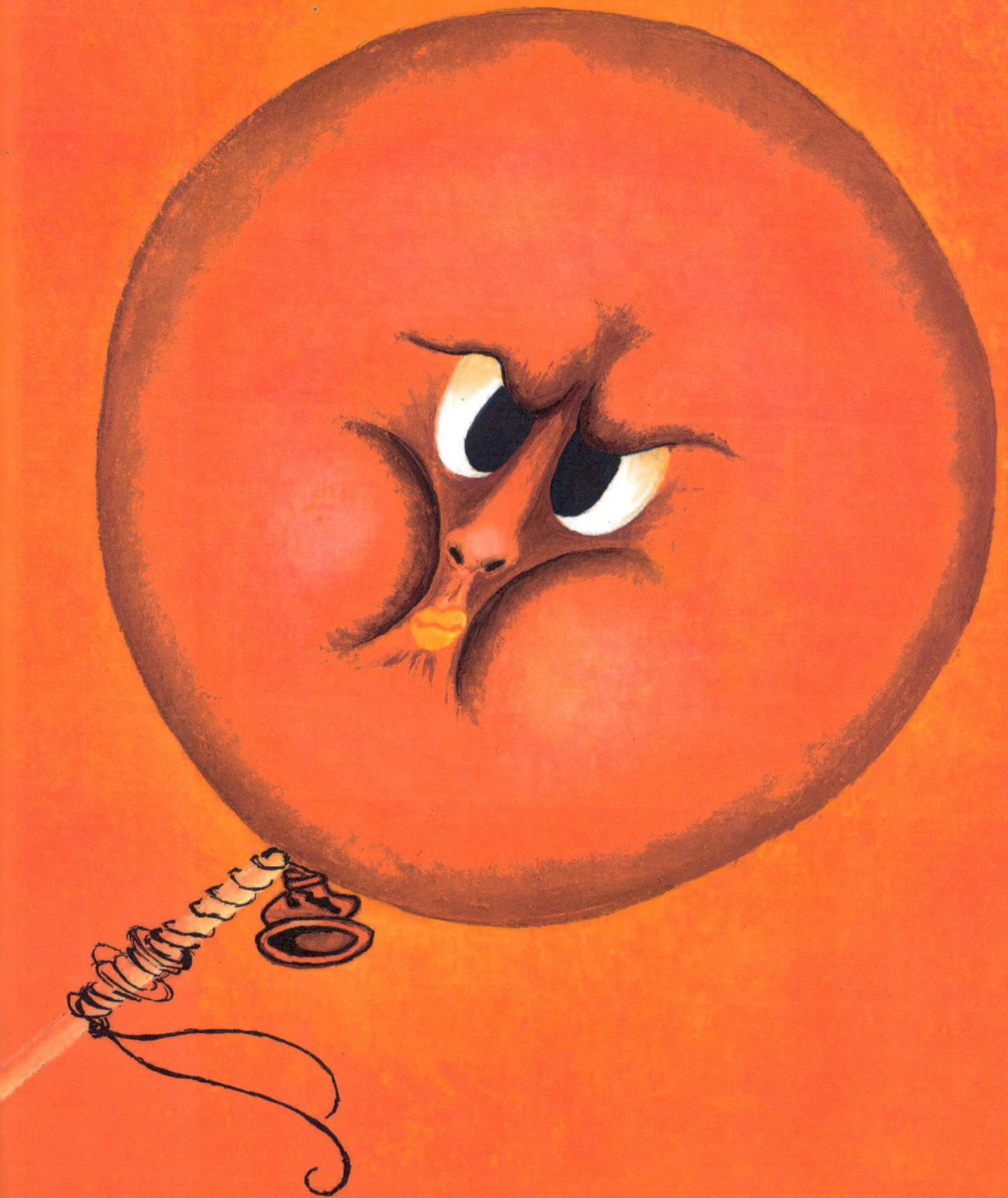

He wished more than anything else

in the whole wide world

that his mum and dad were back together again.

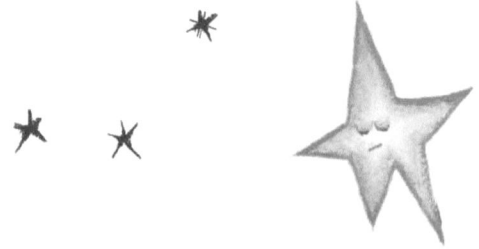

One night Henry had a dream
that his dad had moved back home.

When he realised it was just a dream
he began to cry.

He told his mum how much he missed his dad and that he wanted things back the way they used to be.

Henry's mum gave him the BIGGEST cuddle ever.

She explained that his feelings are a part of grief.

Grief is something that happens to everyone
at different times and for different reasons.

She said, sometimes when a favourite toy is lost or broken, when someone special or a loved pet dies, people grieve.

We also grieve if our family breaks up.

Henry said he didn't like grief
and he wanted it to go away.

His mum said he wouldn't always feel so upset.

Some days he'd forget his sadness altogether.

Henry's mum and dad really really love him. And even though they don't live together anymore, he still has a family.

It's just different now.